50 THINGS I WISH I'D TOLD YOU

LIFE SKILLS

Polly Powell

Illustrated by Laura Quick

PAVILION

Contents

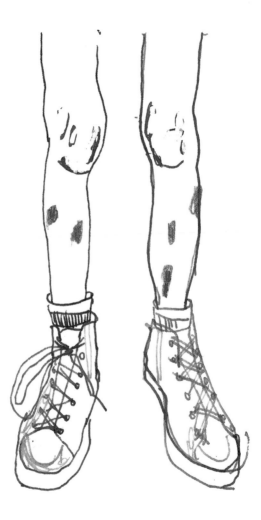

I have two children of whom I am inordinately proud. They have both flown the nest and lead busy, independent lives. But, like every mother, I continue to worry about them. In my mind, I ask myself whether they've had enough food/sleep/love/fun. Or indeed whether they're having too much alcohol/partying/drugs/fun.

This book is cathartic. It is so that I can sleep at night and know that my children have somewhere to turn for helpful advice if I'm not around. It also lets me off the hook for not telling them this stuff in the first place.

To sons and daughters everywhere, don't blame your parents too much for any perceived parenting shortfall — everyone does the best they can. Hopefully, this book can fill the gaps (assuming there are any).

Love Mum x

#1 Be nice to people

The best reason to be nice to people is that it will make them happy, and this in turn will make you feel good about yourself. Helping someone when they drop their shopping, are lost and need directions, or fall over costs you nothing, except perhaps a few minutes of your time, and it will make all the difference in the world to the other person.

Say good morning to security guards and receptionists, smile and thank the people who serve you in shops, bars and restaurants, offer to give up your seat on trains, buses or the tube to people who need it more than you. The warmth you give will be given back to you, not every time, but in time. You will know that you have done the right thing.

Even if your offer of help is spurned, your kindness will ultimately be appreciated. If someone is rude to you, stay calm. You can still assert yourself, and speak your mind, but do so politely. Being the better person is not always easy, but it pays dividends to treat people the way you would like to be treated.

Lecture over.

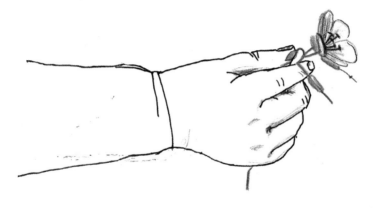

#2 How to make a bed

Flat bottom sheet

1. Lay the bottom sheet onto the bed and adjust it so that it is centrally positioned with an equal amount of fabric at the sides and ends. Smooth it down with your hands.

2. Tuck the sheet firmly under the head end.

3. Tuck the sheet under the foot end, pulling so that there are no wrinkles in the length.

4. Go back to a head-end corner and lift the side sheet up to an angle of around 45° and tuck in the excess fabric that is hanging down.

5. Go to a foot-end corner of the bed and repeat this process. Repeat and repeat.

6. Tuck the sheet in tightly all along one side of the bed. Repeat this process on the other side.

Duvet cover

1. To start, the cover should be inside out.

2. Hold the two head-end corners (from the inside) and match them to the head-end corners of the duvet.

3. Hold firmly and shake so that the cover turns the right way round with the duvet inside. Button up to finish.

Pillow cover

If you can't put a pillowcase on a pillow by now then I have truly failed. I would suggest you marry someone who can.

#3 Five ways to cook an egg

Poached egg

1–2 eggs
Sea salt and black pepper

Bring a saucepan of water up to simmering point;
you do not want it to be boiling hard, just little
bubbles.

Break the egg into a cup or bowl, then gently slip
the egg into the water. Simmer for 2 minutes, then
remove the pan from the heat and let the egg sit
in this water for up to 10 minutes. Spoon a little
water over the top of the egg to help it cook.

Remove the egg from the pan very gently with a
spoon and serve. It's delicious served on a toasted
English muffin with spinach.

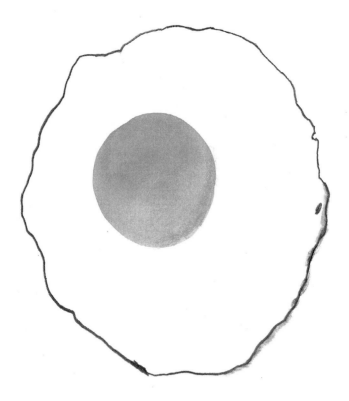

Boiled egg

1–2 eggs
Sea salt and black pepper

For a soft-boiled egg, bring a small saucepan of
water up to the boil and add a pinch of salt. The
water should be deep enough to cover an egg.

Put the egg on a spoon and gently lower into the
water. Turn the temperature down — you want the egg
to simmer, not subject it to a violent boil. Put the
timer on; timing is not a precise science as the age
and size of the egg affect its cooking time. As a
rough guide, 4–5 minutes for a soft, runny egg.

Lift it out with a spoon, and pop into an egg cup
— use a piece of the egg box if you don't have one.
Eat with buttered bread or toast cut into fingers.
Put salt and pepper on the side of your plate and
add to taste a pinch at a time.

For a hard-boiled egg, add to a pot of cold water.
Bring to the boil, then turn down to simmer and cook
the egg for 7 minutes. Remove from the pan and put
into cold running water for a minute. Leave to cool
in cold water. Peel and eat.

Scrambled eggs

3 eggs
Sea salt and black pepper
Knob of butter

Crack the eggs into a bowl, add some salt and pepper
to taste, and whisk up well with a fork. Place a
small non-stick frying pan over a medium heat (eggs
are a pain to clean off a metal pan) and add a knob
of butter. When it's melted and begins to sizzle,
add the eggs. Use a wooden spoon or spatula to stir
the eggs around continuously — the underneath cooks
quickly, so you want to keep moving the egg around
so that it all cooks.

When it's almost done and still a bit runny, lift
the pan off the heat for a moment and give it a good
beat around — it will continue to cook for a few
seconds — so you can assess if it needs more time on
the heat. Keep putting it back on and off the heat
for a few seconds until the texture is perfect for
you. Serve immediately with buttered toast.

Fried egg

1–2 eggs
Sea salt and black pepper
Knob of butter or olive oil

Put a knob of butter, or olive oil, into a non-stick
frying pan and heat gently over a medium heat until
the butter is melted.

Meanwhile, break the egg into a dish (which gives
a neater edge when you tip it into the pan). When
the butter is just beginning to sizzle, slip the
egg gently into the pan. The egg will start to turn
white from the edges first.

If you want the egg sunny-side up, cover the pan
with a lid so that the steam will help cook the top.
Lower the heat and cook gently for 4 minutes for a
runny yoke, 5 minutes for a thicker yolk, or cook
for 6 minutes for a hard yolk. Season with salt and
pepper and serve.

For an over-easy egg, start as before, but when the
edges of the white are set, take a spatula, slide it
under the edge of the egg and flip it over. Cook for
about 1 minute on this side, then season with salt
and pepper and serve.

Remember, if you cook eggs on too high a heat they
will become tough and rubbery.

Basic omelette

3 eggs
Sea salt and black pepper
Chopped chives, tarragon or parsley (optional)
Knob of butter
Filling of your choice (optional)

Crack the eggs into a bowl. Add salt and pepper, and
herbs if you are using them. Beat the eggs until the
yolk and white are mixed together. If you are using
herbs, add them now.

Pop the knob of butter into a frying pan over a
medium heat. As soon as the butter is melted and
just beginning to sizzle, move it around the pan
so that the surface is coated. Pour in the beaten
egg mix. The bottom will quickly begin to set, so
just keep lightly pushing it apart with a spatula
enabling the runny egg on top to slip into the gap.
Lift the omelette up at the sides so that the runny
egg can slip underneath. The middle of the omelette
usually becomes thicker than the edges.

The moment the top of the omelette mix looks moist,
not raw, add your choice of filling. Almost any type
of grated cheese is a good choice — cheddar is an
easy solution, grated Gruyère is delicious, or try a
spoonful of guacamole.

Then tilt the pan, fold the omelette in two and tip
onto a plate. The underside of the omelette should
be a light and golden. Practice makes perfect!

You can also use up any left-over cooked vegetables
and make a sort of Spanish omelette. Just slice and
fry them lightly first so that they are warm, then
add the egg mix and cook as usual.

#4 Eat five portions of fruit and veg a day

Taking care of yourself isn't always easy, but there is one simple rule you should follow: eat five portions of fruit and vegetables daily. Not only will it improve your day-to-day health and boost your immune system, but it may also help you avoid long-term health conditions such as heart disease, type 2 diabetes, strokes, and some cancers, as well as helping you maintain a healthy weight. Here's some advice to help you get your five-a-day:

1. Potatoes don't count! But sweet potatoes, swedes, parsnips and turnips do.

2. No matter how much fruit juice you drink it only counts as one portion of your five-a-day.

3. Dried fruit such as currants and apricots should only make up one portion.

4. Frozen and tinned fruit and veg such as peas, chopped tomatoes and berries all count, but tinned fruit in syrup doesn't.

5. Beans and pulses should only be one portion.

6. All raw fruit and veg count.

7. All cooked veg, except potatoes, add towards your five-a-day. Cooked fruit usually contains added sugar — this reduces the benefits.

#5 Emotional support

Almost everyone you know will go through a tough
time at some point in their lives. Your emotional
support can make a world of difference, but it can
be hard to know how best to help, and what not to do
or to say.

First and foremost, give your friend plenty of time
to talk somewhere private — your job is to listen.
Going for a stroll can be helpful because your
chum can talk without looking at you. Ask open-
ended questions, such as 'What happened', 'What
did you do/say', or 'How did that make you feel'.
Don't interrupt, don't pass judgement and don't be
critical. Whatever you may think of their problem,
it's theirs to deal with, not yours, so don't
minimize how they feel. Show that you understand
their feelings with statements such as 'I'm sorry
that this is happening to you', or 'That would make
me angry, too'.

Your job is not to fix the problem, or to find
solutions, so avoid giving advice. Ask your friend
how they want to deal with the problem. They may not
have an answer yet, but it can be thought-provoking.
Show support in practical ways by taking them out,
or simply by cooking for them. If you are worried,
encourage them to seek professional help.

#6 How to keep a plant alive

Plants need three things to thrive: light, water and food. If your plant has a label, see whether it likes to be in direct sunlight or shade. If the foliage is pale or it's growing fast towards the light, shift it to a brighter position.

Overwatering is the most common mistake, but some plants require more water than others, and how much varies during the seasons. Feel the top of the soil to see if it's wet or dry and, if the soil is pulling away from the sides of the pot, it is too dry. Not all plants like to be watered from above, so the safest method is to stand the plant pot in water in the sink for 15 minutes. When you lift the pot out, let it drain before placing it back in its saucer. If the plant pot is too heavy to lift, pour water into the saucer and see if it disappears — add more until it is no longer absorbed. Don't allow the plant to stand in water in its saucer. Allow plants to dry out a bit between watering, but don't let them get so dry they start to wilt.

Soil will become depleted of nutrients in time; the plant needs most food when it is actively growing in spring and summer. Buy a liquid fertilizer and follow the manufacturer's instructions.

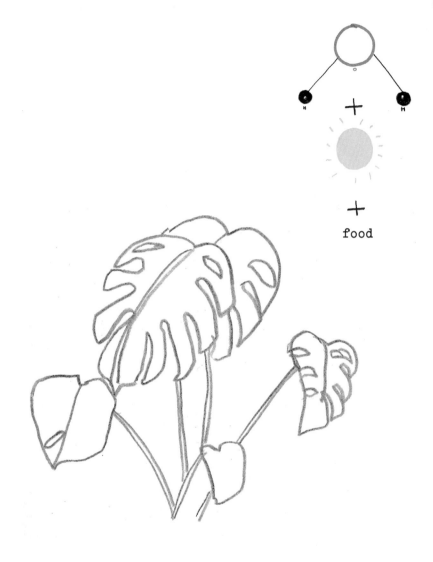

H

O

H

+

+

food

#7 Wrap a present

You'll need either wrapping paper or brown paper
(newspaper can look good), scissors and tape.

If you are wrapping anything fragile or awkwardly
shaped, find a box it will fit into and protect with
tissue paper, or bubble wrap (which of course you
will have saved from a previous online delivery).

1)

On a flat surface, unroll the paper and pop the present onto it. Wrap the paper loosely around it to measure how much paper you need, plus a little extra. Cut this out.

2)

Make a small fold (1cm/$\frac{1}{2}$in) on the right-hand side of the paper to neaten the edge.

3)

Place the present in the centre of the cut paper. Bring the unfolded side up and over the top of the present, then bring the folded side over so it overlaps in the centre. Secure tightly with tape.

4)

Place the present on its narrowest side and push the excess paper down and in at the corners. This will create diagonal folds into the paper ends. Turn the present over and repeat on the other side.

5)

Turn the present so that the taped seam is facing you and flatten the top flap, turn over the cut edge, then lift it to cover the seam on top. Secure with tape. Repeat this process at the other end.

6)

Make the present extra special and decorate with some ribbon and a bow.

#8 Iron a shirt

Most shirts will have a washing instruction label
sewn into a seam. Have a rummage. This should tell
you what the fabric is, so you can set the iron
to the correct temperature. Put water in the iron
reservoir so you can steam iron it — this makes the
job much easier.

Remember, the collar, cuffs and shirt front are
the parts that are most visible, so pay particular
attention to these. Turn the shirt inside out and
always iron on the reverse whenever possible.

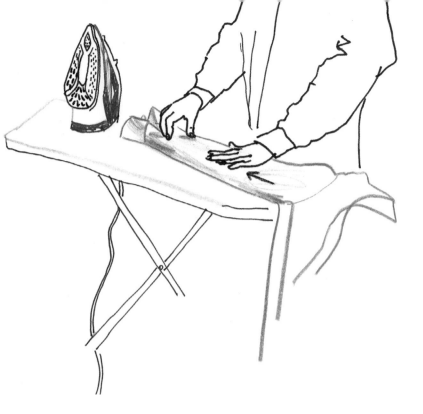

1. Iron the sleeves: Lay a sleeve flat, with the underarm seam closest to you. Run the iron down from the shoulder to the pleats in the cuff, but without going to either edge — you don't want to iron in a crease. Lift up the sleeve and lay it on the board with the underarm seam underneath. Iron up from the underarm seam but do not iron right to the cuff or top of the sleeve.

Press the cuff, moving the iron around the buttons and working from the outer edges inwards so that you don't press creases into the corners.

2. Iron the yoke (the shoulder area): Pop the shirt over the tip of the board and iron, shifting it around until you have done all sections. Iron both sides of the collar, moving from the tip into the centre, as you did with the cuffs.

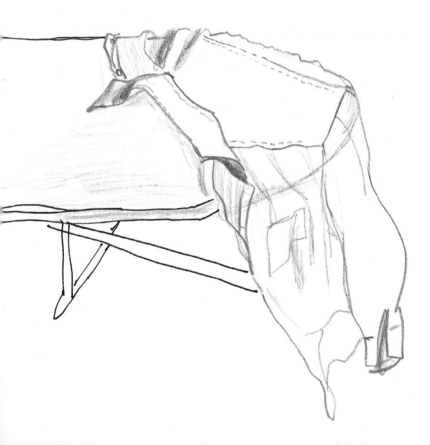

3. Finally, iron the back and fronts of the shirt: Iron the back of the shirt from the yoke downwards and pull the arm away when ironing the seams. For the front, begin by laying the placket (where the buttons and buttonholes sit) straight and press moving around the buttons. Adjust the shirt front and iron the main body of the front.

Most importantly, hang on a hanger.

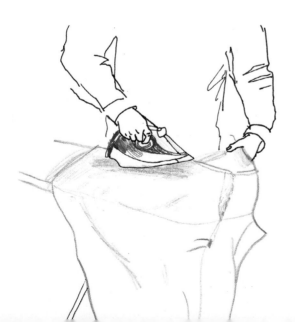

#9 Write a thank-you note

Take the trouble to thank people for their
hospitality, kindness, or generosity — it's just
good manners. The rules are simple: keep it short,
keep it personal, and show appreciation. Write by
hand, do a quick draft so that you know what you
want to say, make sure there are no spelling errors,
and try to keep your handwriting legible. Even if
your note is very late, it is still worth doing, but
if you get into the habit of writing short notes
quickly you'll keep in everyone's good books. A lack
of manners and an absence of thank-you notes may
have been tolerated when you were small, but the
same rules don't apply when you are grown up. An
email or text is better than nothing.

Remember, when someone receives a thank-you note it
makes them smile, and that may be the best reason of
all for sending one.

#10 Mix the perfect Martini

A Martini is the classic cocktail and mixes gin and
dry vermouth (a fortified wine flavoured with aromatic
botanicals) at a ratio of 2:1. The ratios vary
slightly according to preference but you can't go
wrong with this as a starting point. Less vermouth
and you have a dry Martini, more vermouth and you
have wet Martini.

Ice is as important an ingredient as the alcohol,
because a Martini must be arctic cold. Vermouth
should always be kept chilled in the fridge.

Serving a Martini shaken or stirred is also up for
debate; James Bond likes his shaken not stirred (but
then Bond has been known to request a vodka Martini
which some argue is not a Martini at all).

1 serving

60ml/2fl oz of gin

30ml/1fl oz of dry vermouth

Chipped ice

Olives or curls of lemon peel

Equipment

Cocktail glass

Container (for stirred, preferably metal)

Cocktail shaker (for shaken)

Strainer

Chill the gin and cocktail glasses in the freezer for half an hour.

If you opt for stirring, you don't need a cocktail shaker, but you'll need to stir the mix in a chilled container (metal conducts cold) with ice chips for at least thirty seconds.

If you want it shaken, half fill the shaker with ice chips before adding the measures of gin and vermouth. Shake vigorously.

Either way, strain before serving. A Martini is ice cold, not full of ice.

Add a green olive on a cocktail stick and drop it into the glass for a hint of a savoury flavour. Alternatively, add a final flourish with a curl of lemon peel — twist the curl of peel over the top of the glass and run it around the rim of the glass before dropping it in. To make a curl of lemon peel, take a knife and peel the lemon as you would an apple, so you have a long strip of peel.

On a final note — one cocktail is enough, two is one too many, and three is asking for trouble.

#11 Hangover cures

How quickly you get drunk and acquire a hangover
is dependent on factors such as body weight, what
you've been drinking and when you last ate.

<u>Avoidance</u>
The best cure for a hangover is not to drink too
much in the first place. Skip a round every so often
and instead have a glass of water, or a non-fizzy
soft drink to dilute the impact of the alcohol.

Don't drink on an empty stomach. Have a meal that
includes some carbohydrates — pasta, rice, bread,
potatoes — as it slows down the body's absorption
of alcohol.

Drink a pint of water before you go to sleep to
counteract the dehydration caused by the alcohol.

<u>Treatment</u>
Drink fluids that are easy on the digestive system:
water, soda water and isotonic drinks (sports
drinks). A thin vegetable soup, or a stock cube
in boiling water will also help replenish vitamins
and minerals.

Take a painkiller such as paracetamol or ibuprofen,
but avoid aspirin as it won't be good for your
delicate stomach.

Sugary foods can help you feel less weak and trembly.

Try to sleep as much as you can and avoid alcohol
completely for the next 48 hours to give your body
a chance to recover.

#12 How to get a stain out

Most stains can be removed — the secret is to act
quickly before the stain sets (in other words, forms
a chemical bond with the fabric).

If the garment isn't 'dry clean only', treat the
stain immediately with cold water — you can use an
ice cube from your drink or from the freezer. This
will at least remove some of the excess stain and
will help prevent it setting.

Keep fresh stains away from heat and sunlight, as
this enables setting. Note the fabric composition
of the garment before you treat — silk is hardest
to clean. Supermarkets sell specifically targeted
stain removers, but if you don't have them, try the
solutions opposite. If it is a stain like tomato
sauce or curry, try to remove as much of the debris
as possible before you treat it.

Always use a white cloth to work at a stain — an
old ripped-up bit of sheet or a shirt will be fine.
If you use a coloured dishcloth, the chances are it
will just release colour onto your garment, giving
you a separate mark to deal with.

Always place a cloth under the stain, then work from
the back because you want to tease it out of the
fabric, not push it further in. Dab gently, don't
scrub.

Pre-wash treatments

Blood: Rinse with cold water, spot treat with an enzyme cleaner or soak in lukewarm water with detergent and leave for 15–30 minutes before washing.

Grease, fat and oil: Sprinkle with cornflour or talcum powder, give a gentle rub and leave for 15–30 minutes. Brush off and wash as usual. Use a biological washing powder, or try soaking in a dilute dishwasher solution, but wash this out thoroughly as it can bleach.

Red wine: Pour carbonated or warm water over it — bubbles help to lift out the pigment. Apply fine-grain salt and leave for 15–30 minutes before washing.

Tea and grass stains: Apply lemon juice to the area, leave for 15–30 minutes.

Chocolate: Run warm water over the mark, then dab with detergent.

Coffee: Soak in lukewarm water. Dab stain with diluted liquid detergent or vinegar, then wash. Bar soap can set the stain, so don't use it.

Sweat: Soak in warm water, dust with fine-grain salt and leave for 15–30 minutes, or apply an enzyme cleaner.

Mud and dirt: Agitate in lukewarm water to lift the dirt out, put detergent onto the remaining marks and leave for 15–30 minutes.

Urine and faeces: Rinse in cold or cool water, as hot water can set the stain. Soak and agitate in cool water with detergent.

#13 Etiquette

This is just a fancy word for good manners, and these will take you a long way. Here are a few pointers:

1)
Say please and thank you.

2)
Be on time.

3)
Dress appropriately for the occasion whatever your personal style.

4)
Shake hands when you meet someone and introduce yourself.

5)
Make sure you have got someone's name — if you haven't heard, it's fine to ask again.

6)
Look at the person who is speaking to you.

7)
Don't invade other people's space, so keep a polite distance and apologize if you bump into anyone.

8)
Don't turn up to a dinner or a party empty-handed, but don't take anything to a business event.

9)
Wait until everyone has been served before starting to eat.

10)
Remember your table manners (use cutlery from the outside in).

11)
Don't speak with your mouth full.

12)
Remember to ask people about themselves and don't interrupt others while they're speaking.

13)
Don't study your phone in company or at the table, wait until you are alone.

14)
If someone is rude to you, don't respond, as they may be having the day from hell, and it can stop the situation escalating.

15)
Apologize if you are wrong.

16)
Wait 24 hours before responding to an angry text or email. Then respond calmly if you see fit.

17)
Whatever your sex, wait for people to go through doors and hold the door open for them. Thank people when this is done for you.

18)
Let people off trains and buses before getting on yourself.

19)
Clean up after yourself when you are sharing a kitchen or a bathroom.

20)
Knock before you enter someone else's bedroom.

#14 Sewing basics

Sew on a button

Nothing takes the edge off a good look — whatever your style — faster than a missing button.

If your button's hanging by a thread, pull it off before it's lost and tuck it in your pocket for safekeeping. If the button is missing, check the garment's side seams, as manufacturers often sew a spare button onto a label there.

If you don't have any needles and thread, shops sell emergency packs. Find the nearest thread colour match and thread your needle. You want a double length of thread with a knot that ties both threads together at the end. This saves time by giving double strength in one stitch — and, if you're not used to sewing, it prevents you accidentally pulling the thread out of the needle!

Don't sew the button tight against the cloth. If you do this, the button will just ping off again. Buttons need to have a shank — a small length of thread between the cloth and the button that allows a bit of give when it's tugged in day-to-day life.

1. Look for the mark on the cloth where the old button was and sew a knot where you want the new button to sit, leaving the needle and thread attached.

2. Next, take the thread through the button from underneath and take it back down over the top through an opposing hole, down towards the cloth.

3. Put the needle back into the fabric (as close to the knot as possible), make a stitch and pull the thread — the button will come closer and closer to the cloth. Hold the button between two fingers so that it is about 1cm/½in away from the fabric and pull the stitch tight. The button will be hanging loosely, which is what you want.

4. Repeat this process, running the thread through opposing holes in the button until you have at least two stitches through each hole. Each time you tighten your stitch, hold the button the same distance from the fabric. Don't worry if the threads look a bit messy at this point.

5. Now you are ready to finish. With your needle and thread between cloth and button, wind the thread around and around all the loose threads. The shank will get shorter and closer to the cloth as you do this, and the threads will all come together. Put a last stitch into the cloth to secure this binding, then do a couple of loop knots around the shank and snip off the end of the thread.

Take up a hem

This simple blind stitch gives a strong and virtually invisible hem.

1. Get a length of cotton thread. Cut a long length and thread the needle. Tie a knot in one end.

2. If you are repairing a hem, turn the garment inside out and iron press the section that is being re-hemmed. If you are hemming a garment with a raw edge, turn it inside out and press a small hem of no more than $\frac{1}{2}$cm–1cm/$\frac{1}{4}$–$\frac{1}{2}$in. Turn up again and recheck the length. This double turn will hide the raw edge and ensure the hem doesn't fray.

3. Now begin fixing it with tiny stitches. The method of doing this ensures that the stitches hardly show on the outside, and also have a little give if tugged or caught. With the garment inside out, go to where the side seam meets the inside hem. Slip the needle from underneath the side seam (to hide the knot) and make a tiny stitch, then put the needle into the underside of the hem, and make a tiny stitch — go down into the fabric and back out on the same side to catch the fabric. Moving across by about $\frac{1}{2}$cm/$\frac{1}{4}$in for each stitch, put the needle into the main fabric and take a tiny stitch. This will show on the outside of the garment so keep it small.

4. Repeat this process zigging and zagging up and down between the underside of the hem and just above the hem so that it is held in position. As you go, gently pull the thread taut, but not tight; you don't want the stitches to pull. Keep having a quick look at the right side to see if your stitches are showing, they should be barely visible. When you've finished, iron the hem on both sides of the fabric.

#15 How to clean a window

Dirty windows function much like an old grey net curtain, obscuring your view and cutting out the light. Cleaning windows isn't a difficult task, but there is a knack to it — the streaks and smears left behind after cleaning can be more irritating than the dirt ever was.

The best advice is to buy yourself a cheap window cleaning squeegee, which transforms the job. Get a bucket of warm water, squirt in a little washing up liquid, you don't want much foam, or use a window cleaning solution. Alternatively, you can make your own solution by mixing one-part distilled vinegar to one-part water.

Use a sponge to wet the windows and give them a rub — if you use a cloth it will leave lint behind. Shake the sponge every now and then to ensure that any grit is removed. On large windows, move the squeegee in an s-pattern from top to bottom until all the water is lifted off. On multi-pane windows, start at the top and move from left to right and from top to bottom. Periodically wipe the squeegee with a cloth to remove excess water. Wipe the windowsill with a cloth to remove excess water.

Wipe the glass dry with a chamois, or with crumpled-up sheets of newspaper (yes, really).

#16 Cuts and scrapes
(minor first aid)

It's worth having at least a basic first-aid kit
containing plasters, antiseptic wipes, antihistamine
tablets, painkillers, gauze rolls and pads, adhesive
tape and rehydration powders. A bag of frozen peas
wrapped in a tea towel can be used as a makeshift
ice pack.

<u>Blisters</u> Don't pop them! Let them go down by
themselves.

<u>Bruises and swelling</u> Place an ice pack on the
affected area for about 10 minutes. Repeat at
intervals.

<u>Burns</u> Hold under cold running water for as long
as you can bear. If the burn is still painful put
a cold damp cloth over it, cool the cloth down
regularly until the burning sensation begins to
subside. If the burn is bigger than the size of a
large coin see your doctor.

<u>Cuts and grazes</u> Wash your hands (yes, I know) then
apply pressure to the cut for a few minutes with
a clean cloth. Once the bleeding has slowed, wash
the wound with cool water until clean. If there is
any dirt remaining, try to remove it with a pair of
tweezers. Dry the area and cover with a plaster or a
dressing. Remove as soon as practical to let the air
dry the wound. Deep cuts will need to be seen by a
doctor as they may need stitching.

<u>Diarrhoea</u> Drink plenty of water in small, frequent sips. Use an oral rehydration solution to help replace salt, glucose and minerals if you have one. Eat small, bland meals if you are hungry. Stay close to home and near the toilet! Get a chum to buy some anti-diarrhoeal medicine.

<u>Headache</u> Take a painkiller, ideally one with anti-inflammatory properties (ibuprofen) and lie down and try to sleep. Make sure you have a glass of water to drink. Tell someone you are feeling unwell so they can check on you in a couple of hours.

<u>Stings</u> Remove the sting with tweezers if still visible, wash the area to flush away some of the venom, apply an ice-pack, and take an antihistamine tablet. If you need it, take a painkiller. If someone has a severe reaction to a sting seek medical help immediately.

<u>Stye in the eye</u> Don't pop it, apply a clean, warm damp compress 3—4 times a day. It'll sort itself out.

#17 Make a sponge cake

The classic cake. Good to make for your parents
when they come calling. Or a prospective partner.
You will need two 20-cm/7-in sponge tins and baking
paper. If you have a larger cake tin you will need
to make more mix (scale up by adding 1 egg for each
extra 50g/2oz of sugar, butter and flour).

175g/6oz caster sugar

175g/6oz butter, at room temperature

3 eggs

175g/6oz self-raising flour, sifted

Jar of jam

Icing sugar or caster sugar for decoration

Preheat the oven to 180°C/350°F/ Gas mark 4. Grease two sponge tins and line with baking paper.

Put the sugar into a bowl. Cut the butter into small pieces and add it to the sugar. Beat, and beat, and beat some more until you have a soft, pale and fluffy mix. If in doubt, keep beating. Add 1 tbsp of flour and mix in – this helps prevent the eggs from curdling when added to the mix. Break the eggs into a small bowl and whisk with a fork. Add the eggs to the butter and sugar and beat the mix until they are incorporated. Fold the sifted flour in gently until it is mixed in.

Divide the mix between the two tins and spread it out evenly – use a palette knife if you have one. If possible, put both tins on the same shelf in the middle of the oven. Cook for 25 minutes until golden brown.

Once cooled, spread one half with jam (onto the flat side) and gently place the other sponge on top with the flat side down. Sieve a little caster sugar or icing sugar over the top.

#18 Dress codes

Like it or not, your chosen mode of dress sends out
a series of signals which other people interpret.
This applies just as much to people who declare
a complete lack of interest in clothing as it does
to self-declared fashion victims. Social conventions
dictate that in certain situations we should dress
a certain way. Some people kick against this, but
there is no need, because dress codes still allow
for flexibility and personal expression.

Workwear should be smart and comfortable — don't
moan if you have to wear a shirt and tie because,
if it's properly fitted, it will be as comfortable
as a pair of jeans. Shirt collars come in sizes for
a reason! Women no longer have to wear dresses (they
did in my day) and should not be obliged to wear
heels. Keep it smart, avoid anything ill-fitting, too
revealing, see-through or downright shabby — beyond
that, do your own thing.

For smart evening events, men should wear a suit
(and a suit has a thousand interpretations), women
should be smartly dressed and not have too much flesh
on show. Black tie events dictate that men wear a
dark suit or tuxedo with a bow tie (not a regular
tie), women should wear an ankle-length dress,
though shorter evening dresses are OK. White tie is
the most formal social occasion: men are required to
wear a tailcoat with a wing collar shirt and a white
bow tie; women must wear full-length evening dress.
If in doubt always opt for simplicity and decorum.
If you have made an effort you will be forgiven
almost anything!

#19 Paint a wall

First, choose your colour and the 'finish' you
want. Most walls are covered in matt water-based
paint, though kitchens and bathrooms sometimes need
specialist paint if they suffer from condensation.
Buy a couple of small paintbrushes, a roller and
tray, ready-made filler, sandpaper and masking tape.
If you are covering dark paint you will need to buy
a primer (preparatory paint) to paint the walls with
first. Fill any holes in the walls, leave filler to
dry and sand down. Give the wall a wipe over with
a damp cloth, and wipe over the skirting boards.
Make sure you dry them afterwards. Run masking
tape around the skirting boards and the ceiling to
ensure you get a straight edge. Cover the floor with
newspaper, a plastic dust sheet or old curtains you
don't want any more.

Give the paint a good stir, then using a smallish
paintbrush, paint around the skirting board, up the
corners of the room and along the top of the wall,
a process known as 'cutting in'. Pour some paint
into the roller tray, run the roller back and forth
in it, and then back and forth over the tray drainer
to remove excess paint. Run the roller up and down
the walls (professionals use an s-shape motion).
Leave it to dry. Don't panic if the colour looks
darker than you thought, it lightens as it dries.
Apply a second coat with the roller and you should
be done, though some walls may need a third coat.

#20 Colour mixing theory

You might wonder why I have chosen this subject.
Other than the fact that we come from a long line
of artists, I think colour is a crucial ingredient
in how we dress, furnish our homes, and generally
see the world. Colour theory is both an art and
a science, and it explains how colours mix, match
and clash.

A bit of history: it was developed by Isaac Newton
in the 17th century after he discovered that a prism
refracts white light into the colours of the visible
spectrum.

A bit of science: humans see colours in light waves;
data is sent from our eyes to our brain and we
perceive colour.

The primary colours are red, blue and yellow. Mixing
primary colours creates secondary colours — orange,
green and purple. Tertiary colours are created when
a primary colour is mixed with a secondary colour;
if you combine blue and purple you get violet. A
tint is made by adding white to colour, effectively
lightening it. A shade is made by adding black to
your colour, making it darker. A tone is made by
adding grey (a mix of black and white) to a colour.
The human eye can distinguish about 10 million
colours, but the perception of colour is completely
a subjective psychological phenomenon!

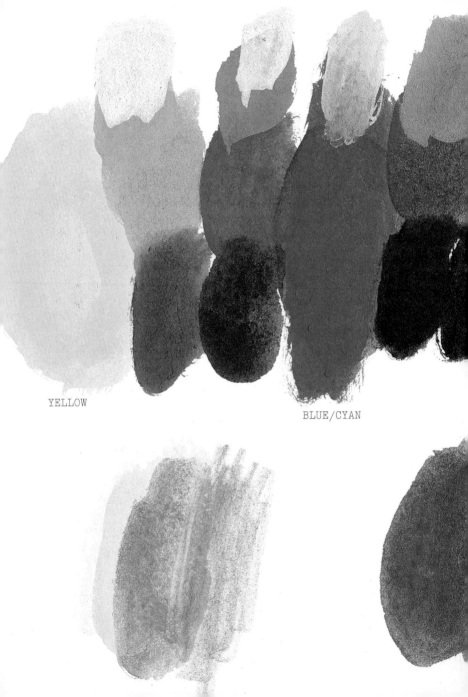

YELLOW

BLUE/CYAN

RED/MAGENTA

YELLOW

#21 Escape a bad date

The mathematical odds are that everyone will have a few bad dates in their lifetime. They can make for very funny stories, but really life is too short!

A simple rule if you are meeting for the first time is to arrange in advance for a quick pre-dinner drink only. If there's zero chemistry you can be polite and pleasant, have one drink, and leave when it's finished. Hold out your hand firmly for a handshake to avoid farewell kisses.

Another strategy is to go the bathroom and call a friend; ask them to call in five minutes and say that there is an emergency and you are needed. Your date will probably know that this is a get-out clause, so just be firm, apologize and leave quickly to save their embarrassment.

If your date is making you feel anxious or unsafe work out a safe escape route. Whatever happens, don't leave with them. If the opportunity arises, be prepared to leave quickly when they visit the bathroom. Or ask for help at the bar — some bars and pubs have a code 'Ask For Angela', when they know that you need assistance. Take the opportunity to discreetly pay for your share of the drinks so that you can leave with a clear conscience and avoid provoking any further ill-feeling.

If your date insists on paying (or pays secretly) you are under NO obligation to reciprocate.

You can say NO at any time.

#22 Is it off?

Assuming your food has been refrigerated, work on
the principle that a use-by date is for guidance
only, with the exception of chicken, pork, fish and
shellfish, which you should bin if it has passed
its best-by date — the smell alone will kill your
appetite.

Fresh beef and lamb should be red. It turns brown
as it ages (you see this clearly with mince), but
it may still be safe to eat. Sniff the meat — if it
smells fine you may be able to use it, just make sure
you cook it thoroughly. If it is whiffy, or if you
are in any doubt, chuck it out.

Vegetables often survive much longer than their use-
by date. The simple test with root veg is to ask
yourself has it gone soft, brown or slippery? If
not, you may be able to use it. If you find a little
bit of brown inside an onion, a clove of garlic, or
a potato, just cut that section out. Some greens
will last for ages — you can chop out any leaves
that are wilted or brown, but don't use anything
that has become slippery or slimy.

Some fruit deteriorates at speed, but a bit of
mildew in a punnet of strawberries or raspberries
doesn't mean the whole lot is spoiled. Remove
anything that is bruised, soft and mouldy, give
what is left a good wash, then eat it quickly!

It's best not to eat mouldy bread — the growth
on the crust is only the tip of the iceberg and
although it probably won't make you ill, it won't
taste very good!

#23 Is it cooked?

A few tips:

Meat
All raw meat carries harmful bacteria so it is
important that it is cooked through thoroughly.

Meat changes colour as it cooks — make sure there is
no red or pink meat left, though good-quality fresh
beef and lamb can sometimes be eaten rare with the
flesh pink. Beef and lamb turn brown, while chicken,
pork and most fish turn whiter.

Pierce the thickest part of the cooking meat with a
skewer, fork or knife; if the juices that run out
are clear it is cooked; if they are pink or bloody
it will need a little longer.

Eggs
The whites should be white and not translucent.
Spoon fat (for a fried egg) or boiling water (for
a poached egg) over the yolk to ensure the whole egg
is cooked through.

Cake
Stick a skewer in the cake, if it comes out clean
with a few crumbs it is done. If there is any
sloppiness it should be returned to the oven.

Press the top lightly with your finger, if it
feels soft but firm and the dent springs back up
it is done.

Pasta and rice
Carefully fish a bit of pasta or rice out of the
pan when you think it's time might be up. Taste
it; pasta should be soft but firm — al dente — rice
should be soft and chewy, not hard.

#24 Clean a bathroom

Snap on a pair of rubber gloves — it will make these grotty tasks more bearable, as well as stopping your skin coming into contact with cleaning fluids. If you've got long hair tie it back.

You'll need:

Rubber/latex gloves
Paper towels
Limescale remover (you can use lemon juice or vinegar)
Drain unblocker (maybe)
Toilet cleaner
Antibacterial cleaner
Bleach (use with caution)

Shower

1. If you have a shower curtain, chuck it into the washing machine with some towels, which help clean the curtain.

2. Remove everything from the shower and rinse it with water to dislodge bits of dirt or hair. Then scoop out all the debris from the drain.

3. Clean the shower in sections, using a cleaning agent with a limescale remover. Leave for 10 minutes before rubbing with sponge. Rinse.

4. Clean the grouting with a mix of 1 part bleach to 2 parts water — use an old toothbrush to get the hard-to-reach places. Rinse.

5. Use limescale remover to clean the chrome parts. Spray the solution, leave for 10 minutes, wipe with a cloth. Rinse. For the shower head,

unscrew it and put it in a plastic bag with some
limescale remover, so the holes are immersed.
Leave to soak overnight. Remember to rinse it and
screw it back on the next day.

6. If your shower is clogged, pour drain cleaner
   into the plughole before you go to bed so that it
   will clear any debris further down the pipe.

7. Open the windows to let the damp air out. Air the
   room often to help prevent the growth of mould.

Loo

1. Flush the toilet. If the toilet is stained, squirt
   bleach around the rim and bowl and leave it
   overnight. Otherwise, just use toilet bowl cleaner
   and leave it for an hour.

2. Spray the cistern and flush handle with an
   antibacterial cleaner and wipe it off with paper
   towels. Pop these straight in the bin.

3. Spray the outside of the bowl and the base with
   antibacterial cleaner and wipe with paper towels.
   Then spray and wipe the lid of the toilet seat on
   both sides. Repeat this with the seat itself, the
   ceramic area underneath and all around the seat
   hinges too.

4. Take a toilet brush and clean around the rim
   of the toilet and down inside it. Holding the
   brush in the toilet, flush it so it cleans in the
   flushing water.

5. If there is still limescale left around the
   rim, spray it with limescale remover and leave
   overnight. Then give it a scrub in the morning
   with a brush.

#25 Hang a picture

This isn't rocket science, but there are a couple
of tricks to making this task straightforward.
You'll need a hammer, picture hooks (one or two-hole
picture hooks depending on weight of artwork), a
tape measure, a pencil and a friend.

Get your friend to hold the picture up to the wall
where you want to hang it, stand back and engage
in an 'up a bit', 'no, left a bit' exercise till
it's in the right position and mark the wall with
a pencil spot at the top centre of the picture.
If you are hanging the picture on a small wall,
then measure the width of the wall and if the pencil
mark isn't slap bang centre, mark the actual centre
point.

Put your picture on a flat surface, pull the wire
taut (as it would be when hanging) and measure the
distance between this point and the top of the
picture. Back to the wall — measure and mark that
same distance down from your centre mark. Take your
picture hook, place the bottom of the hook against
this last mark, and bang the nails in. Hang the
picture and adjust so it sits straight.

SAFETY NOTE: Do check that there are no wires or
pipes in or behind the wall…

#26 Finance

Making ends meet isn't easy and a lot of people get
into difficulties. They put their heads in the sand,
ignore bills, overlook unpaid rent, and increase
their overdraft to the max without once addressing
the issue of their overspending. But the problem
won't go away, and the sooner you face up to it
the better.

The first step is to make a list of your monthly
expenditure. Put in your rent and your monthly
share of the utility bills including gas, water
and electricity. List any monthly payments for
your phone and insurance and don't forget to
include bank and overdraft charges, and credit card
repayments. Work out what you spend a month on food,
travel, petrol, parking, toiletries, clothing and
socializing. Don't just guess, look at your bank
statements and work out what you have actually been
spending. Don't forget income tax or student loans
in your calculations. Add up the total. Now work
out your monthly income. Subtract one sum from the
other and you'll see how much you are overspending
a month.

The next step is to work out how you can cut your
costs. Can you ditch the gym and go running instead?
Could you walk or cycle instead of driving or taking
public transport? Set a limit on what you can spend
on food, clothes and socializing. Can you negotiate
a better tariff from your utility supplier, or a
better phone contract? Use an app to tally what
you are spending and alert you if you are going
over budget. If you have large debts, talk to your
bank and to us, in order to devise a path back to
solvency.

#27 Tipping

There are situations where tipping is expected.
In restaurants and cafés, you are expected to tip
if you have waiter service at the table, 10% is the
minimum you should leave, 15% is more generous,
but you can leave up to 20%. If service charge is
included you do not have to tip, but this may or may
not be passed onto the staff. Don't be embarrassed
to ask as staff are always happy to clarify the
situation. Cash is preferable, but you can ask staff
if tips are passed on when made by card.

Tipping is optional in pubs and bars, but you can
ask the bar person if you can buy them a drink —
they can take this as a drink, or as a tip. If you
are staying in a hotel you should tip the porter
for their trouble, and at the end of your stay
leave some cash for your chambermaid, especially
if you have stayed a few nights and left your room
in a mess. If you have a takeaway meal delivered
tipping is not required, but is much appreciated.
Round the bill up or add a small amount. It is
customary to tip a taxi or cab driver. Round the
bill up, especially if the driver has helped you
with luggage. Tipping the hairdresser is common
practice, 10% is usual, and don't forget the person
who shampooed your hair.

If you are travelling abroad, tipping is common
practice to supplement low wages, and it would be
bad manners not to do so. Check online before you
travel as what is expected varies from country to
country.

#28 Mending a bicycle puncture

Release the brakes and remove the bicycle wheel
either by using the wheel release levers or by
unscrewing the nuts with a spanner.

Remove the cap from the inner tube valve and remove
the valve nut — put them somewhere safe.

Place the thin end of tyre levers between the tyre
and the rim and pop the tyre over the rim — start at
the opposite side to the valve.

Loosen the tyre on one side only and remove the
inner tube.

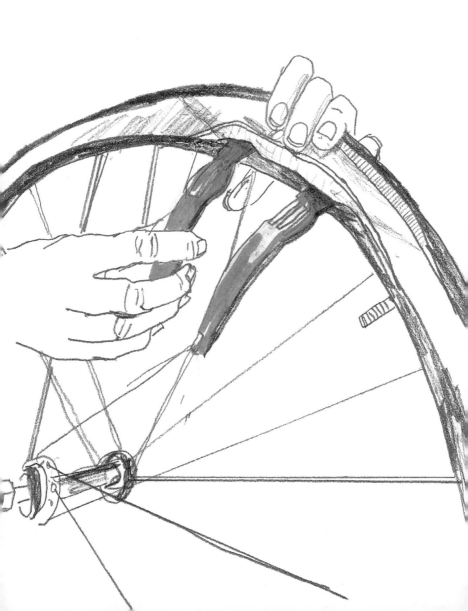

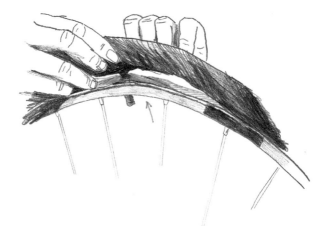

Pump the inner tube up and listen for hissing.
Alternatively, place pumped-up sections of the inner
tube into a basin of water and look for bubbles to
reveal the position of the puncture.

Mark the hole with chalk from the repair kit and dry
the area.

Gently roughen the puncture area with sandpaper from
the repair kit. Apply glue, allowing a good margin
of adhesive beyond the area of the puncture.

When the glue is tacky, peel the backing off the
repair patch and put it into position; press and
hold it in place for a minute. Leave the top cover
in place until you are confident the glue is dry,
then peel it gently away. Dust the gluey area with
chalk.

Pump the inner tube up to make sure the puncture
repair is sound.

Partially inflate the inner tube and replace it
starting with the valve and taking care not to
twist it.

Hook the tyre beading back onto the wheel rim,
starting with the valve. The last bit is tricky —
roll the tyre onto the rim and make sure the inner
tube isn't caught in a pinch. Replace the valve nut,
inflate the tyre and replace the cap. Refit the wheel
and reconnect the brakes.

#29 Digital manners

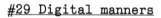

It's very easy to write something contentious or offload your feelings online in the heat of the moment: it can lose you friends, a job, and damage your reputation.

Never, ever, write anything in an email that you wouldn't say to someone's face, especially at work. You may have pressed the delete button, but the mail will still sit on the system. In some countries, everyone at work has the right to apply for digital disclosure to see all electronic communication in which their name has been referenced. Your emails will resurface.

By the same token, never put anything on social media about anyone either at work, or in your personal life, without first checking it's OK. Posting a picture of someone drunk, streaking, revealing the first glimpse of a wedding dress, or news of someone else's pregnancy may not go down well.

Remember that potential employers routinely check out social media, so you may want to think about removing that provocative bikini shot that your friends loved or deleting shots of the morning after the night before!

Don't constantly check your phone at work. Respond when you take a break and put your phone out of sight. People will assume you're not working and judge you. Don't fiddle constantly with your phone on a date or in company, and especially not at mealtimes. Enjoy the company of the people you are with.

#30 How to put up a tent

There are numerous designs of tent on the market
and all have their own instructions. These are
as precious as rubies — do not lose them. Practice
putting the tent up a day or two before you go
on your first camping trip.

Choose a flat site, ideally with some shelter and
away from trees. Check the area over for any
stones and twigs and sweep them away — they'll
make sleeping uncomfortable and can pierce the
groundsheet. First lay out your groundsheet, then
lay your tent on top of it, making sure the entrance
is facing the way you want it to — ideally away from
the wind. Put a few pegs into the ground to secure
it temporarily.

The next stage is to insert the poles into the tent
frame and raise the tent (this is the fiddliest bit).
If you have snap-poles put them together working
from the centre outwards. Adjust the poles to make
the tent as taut as it can be — you don't want it to
flap in the wind. Redo the tent pegs so the guy ropes
are good and tight, they should not be pegged close
to the tent, but at a distance to aid stability.
Angle tent pegs and use a mallet or a rock to hammer
them in on the slant — never try to do this with
your foot — that can lead to a visit to A & E.

Essential extras:
Torch or wind-up light
Mallet
Spare tent pegs

#31 The perfect handshake

This is a small part of any introduction, but it forms an immediate impression, so it's important to get it right. A strong handshake indicates self-confidence, a weak, limp-wristed handshake hints at insecurity, and if you release a handshake too quickly it suggests arrogance.

From a distance of about 1m/3ft from the person you are meeting, look them in the eye, say hello, or good morning/afternoon/evening clearly, and extend your right arm, slanting your fingers slightly downwards and thumb up. This is proffering a greeting. Lift your hand to meet the other person's palm and wrap your fingers and thumb around their hand as though they are hugging it. Do not squeeze their hand so tightly that it is the shake equivalent of bear hug, nor let your fingers just sit against their hand like limp hotdogs. This should be a comfortable, firm and friendly hand hug. While you are doing this maintain eye contact. Shake the hand three times then release. If your hands are sweaty or dirty, wash them in advance of a meeting and keep a handkerchief in your pocket so you can give them a quick and subtle wipe.

#32 How to bake brownies

220g/8oz butter

100g/3½oz
dark chocolate,
broken into
chunks

100g/3½oz
plain flour

1 tsp salt

2 tsp baking
powder

450g/16oz
caster sugar

4 large eggs
beaten

100g/3½oz
pecans or
walnuts,
roughly chopped
(optional)

100g/3½oz
chunks of
white chocolate
(optional)

Preheat the oven to 180°C/350°F/
Gas mark 4.

You'll need a baking tray measuring
approximately 33 x 23cm/13 x 9in,
greased and lined with baking
parchment.

Melt the butter and chocolate
gently in a saucepan, remove from
heat as soon as it is melted. Sieve
the flour, salt and baking powder
into a bowl, mix together with the
sugar, add the melted chocolate and
butter, and then the eggs. Mix well
to combine. If you are using nuts,
add them now.

Pour the mix into the tray and
place on a shelf in the centre of
the oven. Cook for 30 minutes but
check after 25 minutes if you're
not used to your oven. The brownie
should have a light crust on the
outside, but the inside should be
gooey and sticky. The worst mistake
you can make is to overcook a
brownie.

Leave the brownies to cool in the
tin before removing.

#33 How to tie a tie

Someone once said that a tie is just a giant arrow,
but ignore that.

Four-in-hand knot

1)
Turn your shirt collar up
and do up the top button.

2)
Hang the tie around your
neck with the thick end
on your right. This end
should be pulled down so
it hangs around 30cm/12in
below the thin end.

3)
Taking the longer length
in your hand, loosely
wrap it twice across the
thinner length.

4)
Now tuck the wider end of
the tie underneath the
loop at the back of the
tie and push it upwards.

5)
Hold the thick end of the
tip of the tie in your
fingers and insert it down
through the front loop of
the tie, then gently pull
through.

6)
Hold the thinner length
of the tie taut with one
hand, and hold the 'knot'
in your other hand, and
slide the knot gently
upwards.

7)
Adjust the knot so that
it is at the centre of
the collar, then turn
down your shirt collar.

#34 Nose picking and other habits

We all have bad habits, but the question is should
we inflict them on others? The simple answer is no!
What you have to remember is that you will make
other people feel physically sick and do you really
want to repulse your nearest and dearest or even
complete strangers for that matter?!

If you really have to pick your nose do it in
private (and yes people can see you picking your
nose in the car). Worse still is picking your nose
and eating the excavated contents. Nose picking
introduces all the germs on your fingers and under
your nails to your mouth and can make you ill — you
may as well go around licking door handles — it
amounts to the same thing.

Spitting used to be socially acceptable, and it
still is in some countries. But not here! Gobbing is
only just about tolerable amongst athletes, but at
no other time is it attractive or desirable. Nail
biting, as with nose picking, can make you sick
by introducing germs to your mouth. It can also
permanently damage the nail tissue. Keep your nails
short to discourage biting and notice when you bite
so that you understand what triggers the habit.

Farting in public is simply unacceptable. Apologize
if it happens accidentally.

#35 Keep someone alive
(major first aid)

Your job is to keep the person safe until professional help arrives.

1)
Always protect yourself first — is there any danger to you?

2)
Assess the situation: how many casualties are there, what has happened, how old are the people involved?

3)
Call the emergency services. Only move the injured person(s) if the situation isn't safe.

4)
Try to be calm. If there are a number of casualties, prioritize the person who has the worst injuries first.

5)
If the patient is unresponsive, check their breathing and pulse. If they are unresponsive and not breathing, you need to do CPR (see opposite).

6)
If the person is responsive, introduce yourself, find out their name and what has happened. Ask if they are in pain, if they have any allergies or are on any medication, if they have any existing conditions and when they last ate.

7) Are they bleeding or injured? If they are bleeding, apply pressure to the wound — if there is anything embedded in the wound, don't remove it, instead apply pressure around the object. Don't be afraid to shout for help.

CPR (cardiopulmonary resuscitation) if unresponsive and not breathing

Always call the emergency services first. Put the patient on their back. Using the heel of the palm of both hands, push down in the centre of the chest, pumping up and down 100–120 times per minute — faster than once a second. Stop, lift the chin, open mouth and check airway isn't obstructed. Resume chest compressions. Continue in this way until help arrives.

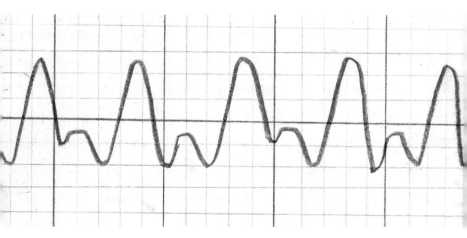

#36 Online safety

The internet is a fabulous tool but stay safe when using it.

- Always make sure your security software is up-to-date not only on your PC, but also on tablets and smart phones to avoid infection by malware.

- Be careful what you post on social media. Avoid posting any material that you would not be happy for a potential employer to see — it's common practice for companies to search for you. Information posted on social media can be used in identity theft.

- Never give away information online that reveals your address or car registration.

- Change your passwords regularly and do not use the same password for numerous websites. Note them down but do not keep them near the computer.

- If in doubt about an email, post or text, do not open it, delete it. Look out for phishing attacks and don't reveal any personal or financial information in unsolicited emails. These emails can look like genuine requests for information, but do not respond — they will try to steal your information. Contact the company directly to check if the email is legitimate.

- Use safe payment options when online shopping.

- Limit the business you conduct in Wi-Fi hotspots; avoid logging into emails or doing online banking because these locations will not be secure.

#37 How to clean clothes and shoes

Cleaning clothes
Getting to grips with laundry can be daunting.
Always check the temperature a garment should be
washed at before you begin. Hunt around the inside
seams and you will find the washing instructions.
Cotton and linen fabrics can take a 40°C/104°F
wash, man-made fibres are safest washed at around
30°C/86°F. Wool should be done on a cool wash.

Never underestimate the power of stain removers
— see #12 for some pre-wash treatments. Sort
your whites, pales, colours and darks and wash
separately. If you don't have this luxury, mix
whites with pales or colours with darks to avoid
colour runs.

Cleaning shoes
Start by cleaning off any dirt from the sides of the
sole with water and a cloth. Leave the shoes to dry.

Leather: Apply a matching colour shoe polish with a
soft cloth. Then use a soft brush to rub vigorously
back and forth until you get a shine. Follow up with
a polish from a cloth.

Suede: Buy a suede cleaning device which has several
different faces which help to remove dust and dirt,
marks and to brush the nap.

Canvas: Clean the sides of the soles with a mix of
equal parts baking soda and water and use an old
toothbrush to work it into the ridges. Remove the
laces and put the sneakers into the washing machine.
Wash at a low temperature with half the detergent
you would usually use. Leave the shoes to dry
naturally.

#38 First apartment

Renting your first apartment is exciting, but don't get carried away with the first place you see, however desperate you are. If something annoys you or worries you now, the chances are it will become a major irritant when you move in.

Check out the areas you are happy to live in, where you feel safe and with convenient public transport links. If you find somewhere you like you'll need to be prepared to snap it up quickly, so make sure you have thought how you will pay the deposit (which may be required by the landlord) and the first month's rent in advance. Work out what you can afford to pay. If you are renting as a group, ask for their budget limit.

Check out what is included in the rent; any utility bills, a cooker, refrigerator, washing machine, and furniture. Establish what heating system is installed and check to see if the locks are secure. Ask whether you are allowed to decorate. If there is a garden, can you use it and are you responsible for its maintenance? Are the communal areas well maintained? Ask the rental agent or current housemates about the landlord, and how repairs are dealt with. Find out how loud or quiet the area is, though you should expect to respect quiet times.

Remember to cook a sponge cake and ask your parents over, however squalid the set-up.

#39 Bills

Living independently is a rip-roaring adventure,
but brace yourself, as you will also be liable for
your share of the bills: electricity, water, gas if
you have it, and local government taxes. Remember,
whoever's name is registered for these is liable for
the cost of paying the bill, so if anyone refuses
to make a payment, or does a bunk (and the nicest
friends do this to their chums) you will have to pay
their share. If possible, make sure everyone's name
is registered, or at least two names so you are not
solely responsible.

You can shop around to get the best deal possible
from different utility companies, but not all
landlords allow you to do this. A monthly bank
transfer is the safest payment method as it spreads
costs out evenly and helps you budget a meagre
income. Your electricity and gas bills can be
adjusted quickly if you are paying too much or too
little. You may be able to pay gas, electricity and
water bills in quarterly arrears. If you have oil-
fired heating, you'll have to pay to have your oil
tank refilled in advance.

If you fall behind with any bill it will affect
your credit rating so, if you are having problems,
deal with it straight away. Speak to the companies
concerned and talk to an organization that offers
free legal advice.

#40 Dance the waltz

The waltz is danced to three beats in four rhythm, with the emphasis on the first beat; <u>One</u> two three, <u>one</u> two three …

The box step is the simplest to learn and partners mirror each other's movements. Start with your feet together.

<u>Lead step</u>

Place right hand on partner's back, hold their hand with your left hand.

1. Step straight forward with LF, heel to toe.

2. Step forward with the toe of the RF so that the RF is parallel to the LF.

3. Bring toe of LF to meet the RF, drop heels.

4. Step straight back with RF toe first, then heel.

5. Step back with the toes of the LF so that the LF is parallel to the RF.

6. Bring the toe of the RF to meet the LF. Drop heels.

<u>Follow step</u>

Place left hand on partner's shoulder, hold their hand with your right hand.

1. Step straight back with the RF toe first.

2. Step back with the toe of the LF so that the LF is parallel to the RF.

3. Bring toe of RF to meet the LF, drop heels.

4. Step straight forward with the LF heel first, then toe.

5. Step forward with the RF toe first so that the RF is parallel to the LF.

6. Bring the toe of the LF to meet the RF. Drop heels.

#41 Four simple pasta recipes

The Italians serve their pasta al dente — 'to the
tooth' — which means it is cooked just long enough
to be neither crunchy nor soft, but chewy and firm.
Try the spaghetti after it has been cooking for
6 minutes: hook a bit out and bite it. It will
probably still be rather crunchy, keep trying
another strand every 30 seconds until you can tell
it is just cooked enough. Remember that different
types of pasta require different cooking times.

1   2 3   4

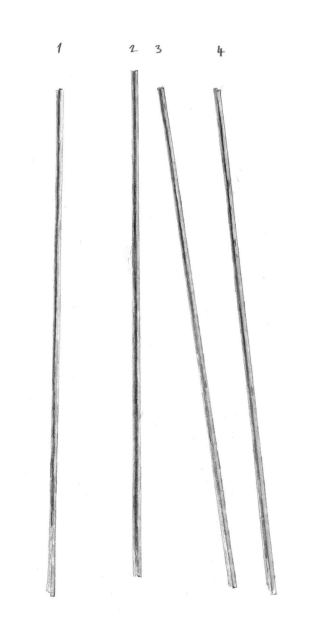

Spaghetti Carbonara

This is made in the time it takes to cook the spaghetti. The secret is to make just enough pasta for each person so that it is all coated with lots of lovely sauce. Serves 4.

450g/1lb spaghetti

40g/1oz butter (or you can use olive oil)

130g/4oz of *cubetti di pancetta* or 4–6 rashers of bacon chopped into small squares

1–2 cloves of garlic, diced

3 eggs

Sea salt and black pepper

Coarsely grated parmesan

Bring a large pan of salted water to the boil, then add the spaghetti. Check the cooking time and set a timer.

Put the butter in a frying pan. When melted, add the pancetta cubes or the diced bacon and cook gently over a medium heat until browned. Then add the garlic and cook for another minute.

Break the eggs into a bowl, season, and beat so the yokes and whites are mixed. Put on one side.

When the pasta is cooked, drain it into a colander and quickly pop it straight back in the same saucepan, but do not put it back on the heat.

Empty the bacon and butter from the frying pan into the saucepan with the pasta, give a quick stir, then add the beaten eggs. Stir this around until you get a lovely, creamy sauce. Sometimes you have to pop the saucepan back on the heat for a moment or two but do this gently and only briefly or you'll have scrambled eggs with spaghetti! Serve onto plates, season with more black pepper and some coarsely grated parmesan.

Aglio Olio Peperoncino

This dish (basic translation — garlic, oil and chili)
comes from Rome and is incredibly tasty! It's simple,
but needs to be well done. If you overcook the pasta
or burn the garlic and chili it will be spoiled.
Serves 4 as a starter; 2–3 as a main course.

450g/1lb
spaghetti

6 cloves of
garlic

1 chili — very
hot

About 5–6
tablespoons
extra virgin
olive oil

Chopped fresh
parsley
(optional)

Coarsely grated
parmesan
(optional)

Bring a large saucepan of salted
water to the boil and add the
spaghetti. Give it a good stir
and cook al dente.

While the pasta is cooking, gently
cook the cloves of garlic, peeled
but not chopped, and the finely
chopped chili in the oil over a
medium heat for one to two minutes
— whatever you do, don't burn
the garlic as this will ruin the
flavour.

When the pasta is cooked, spoon a
couple of tablespoonfuls of the
water into the frying pan with the
garlic and chili.

Drain the pasta, return to the
saucepan and pour over the contents
of the frying pan, stirring around
so all the pasta is coated and
serve.

Some people like a little freshly
chopped parsley or parmesan.

Spaghetti Bolognaise

Serves 4.

1 onion

1 carrot

1 stick of
celery

Extra virgin
olive oil

1–2 cloves of
garlic, crushed

1–2 chicken
livers

65g/2½oz
*cubetti di
pancetta*

450g/1lb minced
beef

2 x 400g/
14-oz tins
chopped
tomatoes

70g/2½oz/tomato
purée

Sea salt and
black pepper

450g/1lb
spaghetti

Coarsely grated
parmesan
(optional)

Dice the onion, carrot and celery.
In a saucepan, fry the vegetables
gently in oil over a medium
heat. When the onion is soft and
translucent, add the garlic.

Chop the chicken livers finely and
add to the pan with the pancetta.
Cook for a few minutes, then add
the minced beef. Give it a good
stir to mix the mince up with the
vegetables. Stir occasionally so
all the meat cooks.

Add the chopped tomatoes and the
tomato purée, season, stir, and
bring up to a simmer. Once the
sauce is simmering, cover the pan
with a lid and cook at a low heat
for about 30–40 minutes, then take
the lid off and cook for another
30–40 minutes. Have a taste to see
if you have added enough seasoning.

About 20 minutes before the sauce
is ready to eat, bring a large
saucepan of salted water to boiling
point, add the pasta and cook for
the required length of time. Drain
and serve the pasta on plates,
adding dollops of sauce on top.

Some people like it with grated
parmesan on top.

Pasta with a tomato, cream and mushroom sauce

This is the ultimate comfort food — it's cheap and easy, requiring little in the way of preparation. Serves 4 as a starter; 2–3 as a main course.

1 onion sliced	Slice the onion and cook gently in olive oil in a saucepan over a
Olive oil	medium heat.
1 clove of garlic, crushed	When the onion is soft and translucent, add the crushed garlic and cook for another minute. Chuck
2 x 400g/ 14-oz tins chopped tomatoes	in the chopped tomatoes, the double cream and the tomato purée.
	Add the sliced mushrooms to the sauce. Give everything a good stir,
170ml/6fl oz/ double cream	season with salt, and bring up to simmer.
70g/2½oz tomato purée	Leave the sauce simmering gently for 40 minutes to thicken and reduce.
250g/8oz white mushrooms, thickly sliced	About 20 minutes before the sauce is ready, heat a pan of boiling salted water, cook the pasta al
Sea salt	dente, drain and serve on plates. Put the mushroom sauce on top. This
450g/1lb pasta of your choice	tastes even better the next day!

#42 Locked out of the house

Most of us will do this at least once in our lives.
Easy solution: give a spare key to a neighbour or
friend you trust <u>now</u>.

If you share a house, get all your housemates'
telephone numbers from day one so you can contact
them in an emergency. Similarly, when you move
in somewhere, pop around to the neighbours and
introduce yourself, so that if you are ever caught
in a lock-out situation they will be much more
amicable if they already know you.

Walk around the house and check all the windows and
doors. They may all look closed, but one may not
have been properly shut. If an upstairs window is
open, you'll need to borrow a ladder — good luck
with that. If no windows are open, and you have no
phone on you, go straight around to a neighbour.
If it is the middle of the night they may not be
thrilled to be disturbed, but neither will they
want you to come to any harm because they ignored
your plea for help. They can help you track down a
locksmith and give you somewhere safe and warm to
wait for their arrival.

A locksmith will want to be paid up front, so if you
don't have the funds this is the time to call the
bank of mum and dad. However much grief you may be
given, we'll help you out, even if you are expected
to repay the debt. Fees vary, so if possible, call
around and find out who can actually come out, and
what the total charge will be. Smashing windows and
breaking down doors are for emergencies only.

#43 How to pack

There is no standardized international carry-on suitcase size or weight, so check with your airline what the maximum dimensions are and what weight is allowed. Make a list of what you want to take and be ruthless. If you haven't worn that dress or shirt for the last three summers will you really wear it this summer?

1)
If you have a carry-on case your toiletries cannot contain more than 100ml of liquid, so buy small plastic bottles and decant your favourite products in them. Put them in a clear bag for security. Buy everything else on arrival.

2)
Put shoes, soles together, in a plastic bag and pack at the bottom of your case. You can stuff your shoes with socks.

3)
Fold flat shirts, trousers and skirts and either roll them up, or lay them at the bottom of the case.

4)
Roll up underwear, T-shirts and socks to maximize space and minimize wrinkles, and tuck into spaces.

5)
Wear your heaviest shoes to travel in.

6)
Keep an emergency set of clothes in your hand luggage in case your checked-in suitcase goes missing in transit.

#44 How to light a fire

To make a fire successfully you need: 1. tinder
— dry materials that will ignite with a spark;
2. kindling, such as small twigs; 3. wood, the
sustaining fuel, in a mixture of sizes; and
4. matches. (You can of course use firelighters.)

If you are lighting a wood-burning stove or
fireplace, first check that any air vents are open,
as you want the chimney to draw the air up. If there
is no draft, the fire will be reluctant to start. If
there is any ash left from a previous fire, clear it
away because you want as much air circulating as
possible.

First, make a nest of tinder — if you are using
newspaper, scrunch it up into loose balls of
paper. Put the kindling on top, leaving spaces of
under 1cm/½in between the sticks. If you are using
firelighters, place them amongst the kindling —
if you don't have firelighters, use more scrunched-
up newspaper instead. Place smaller pieces of wood
around the kindling in an upwards tepee formation,
saving the big chunks of wood for when the fire has
got going. Now put a match to the firelighters or
the upper pieces of newspaper. When you have a good
blaze going you can add the larger logs. When these
are burning hard, reduce the draft so that the wood
doesn't burn too fast.

#45 How to put out a small fire

Don't panic. This is the time for a quick and calm response. If in doubt, always call the fire brigade.

<u>Electrical fires</u> Don't mess around, call the fire brigade. If safe to do so, switch off the power at the socket and close appliance doors to cut off the oxygen supply. If you have a fire blanket, place it gently on top of the fire.

<u>Pots and pans</u> If the contents of a saucepan are on fire, use an oven glove to safely put the saucepan lid on top to cut the oxygen supply (or use a metal tray). Wearing the oven glove, gently remove the pan from the heat. You can use a fire extinguisher on grease or oil fires — always direct the extinguisher at the base of the fire and not at the flames. Never use water on fires fuelled by oil or grease as it will make things much worse.

<u>Gas fires</u> If possible, turn off the gas supply at source. Use a fire extinguisher, directing the spray at the base of the fire.

<u>Smoke</u> If there is smoke, call the fire brigade. Shut doors and get everyone out of the building as quickly as possible. If you are in a flat, set off the fire alarm and alert people on other floors if it is safe to do so.

<u>Camp fires that are under control</u> Let them die down as much as possible, then pour water gently over the fire and make sure it is properly extinguished before leaving it.

#46 Feeling blue

Feeling blue is something we all experience at times and is a natural reaction to difficult circumstances, such as the break-up of a relationship, bereavement, disappointment, bullying or financial pressures. Your natural inclination may be to hide away from people, to dwell on your misery, and neglect yourself. Try not to brood. You can end up isolated, lonely and feeling much, much worse.

You need to be kind to yourself. Moderate aerobic exercise three times a week stimulates the release of endorphins and other feel-good chemicals in the brain. You don't have to start running, as a brisk walk in the park or by a river will do as well. Look at the world around you, live in the moment. Yoga is helpful too, as it lessens levels of stress and anxiety and promotes well-being.

Talk to people you trust, and seek out friends with a positive attitude. If you are feeling unsociable meet people on your own terms, go for lunch or a quick drink rather than being dragged to a wild party. Eat healthily and don't seek consolation in alcohol or other stimulants. By the same token, avoid sad films or books, and only watch or read things that have a feel-good factor. Address any issues that are making you feel sad, such as a bad relationship or a miserable job, and take control. If your feelings persist, or if you have any thoughts of self-harm, seek professional help. You are unwell.

Depression is no different to any other illness and there is no shame in owning up to how you are feeling. Be your own best friend and take care of yourself.

#47 Small talk

Chatting to strangers in a social situation can be daunting. Remember that almost everyone else feels the same, and most people are happy that someone else has approached them.

The first thing to do is to pick out people who are alone, or those that seem the least intimidating. Go up to them, smile broadly, say hello and introduce yourself. People nearly always respond in kind. Try to remember their names.

Once you've broken the ice, follow up with an open-ended question (one that doesn't have a yes/no answer). If you are at a work function you could ask the other person what brings them here (hoping you are not speaking to the host of the event). People love talking about themselves, so listen to what they are saying, respond, and ask more questions. If they seem bored, or unwilling to chat, or they are crashing bores, excuse yourself after a few minutes.

If you're at a party you can ask how people know each other, how they know the host, or what they do. These may not be the most inspiring questions, but they get the ball rolling. Don't take it personally if people aren't willing to talk, they may have been in the middle of a whispered argument with their partner, or catching up on some riveting gossip.

#48 The perfect cup of tea and coffee

Tea

Never use water that has already boiled. Empty the kettle and let the water run so it is well oxygenated, then fill the kettle.

- Before the kettle has boiled, warm the pot — or indeed the cup if you can't be bothered with teapots — by swilling hot water around it.

- Loose-leaf tea is best. Bigger teabags are better than smaller ones as they allow the tea to circulate. Alternatively, opt for a strainer.

- The water temperature is important and some kettles have adjustable settings. Black teas should be brewed in water at 96°C/204°F, green teas at around 70°C/158°F.

- Use one small spoon of tea per person and one for the pot.

- The optimum brewing time varies according to the type of tea — check the packet for instructions.

- Tea tastes best drunk from a porcelain cup as it does not affect the temperature or taste — you can pick these up cheaply from vintage shops.

- If you make tea in a pot you can add the milk to the cup before or after you pour the tea. But if you make tea in a cup, add the milk afterwards, so the tea can brew at the correct temperature. Never squeeze teabags as it brings out the tannins and affects the taste.

Coffee

Whether you use the filter system (drip coffee makers), a cafetière (French press) or a full-scale coffee maker, the rules for getting the perfect cup are the same:

- Buy freshly roasted coffee beans. Coffee tastes best within 5–7 days of being roasted, though the flavour can remain consistent for up to a month.

- Store coffee beans in airtight containers to keep them fresh.

- Buy good coffee beans. Arabica beans, the most expensive, are considered to be the best.

- Grind your own coffee — beans ground immediately before brewing produce the best flavour. Clean your grinder after every use. A finer grind extracts more of the coffee's flavour; a coarser grind contains more of a caffeine hit.

- Use fresh water. If your water tastes chlorinated, use spring water or filter your water.

- Good coffee requires a brewing temperature of about 96°C/205°F, so after the kettle has boiled let it sit for about 30–45 seconds to drop to the right temperature. If the water is boiling it makes the coffee taste more bitter.

- The standard measure is about 2 tbsp of a ground coffee for a 6-oz cup.

- When using the filter system, buy oxygen bleached or 'dioxin-free' filter papers.

- When using a cafetière, pour the water over the grounds and let it steep for 30 seconds, then give it a stir. Let it sit for 2 minutes before pushing the filter to the bottom.

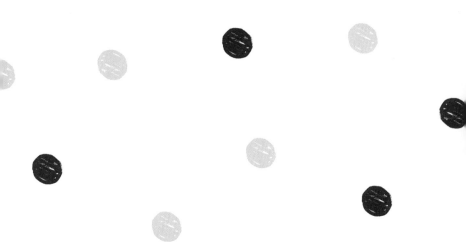

#49 Put it down to experience

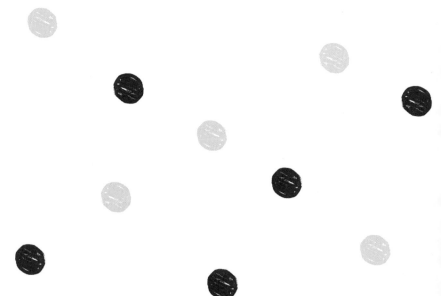

'Experience is not what happens to you; it's what you do with what happens to you.'
Aldous Huxley

Everyone gets knockbacks in life; what counts is what you take from the experience. It's perfectly normal to feel down when something goes wrong, and though it may feel like the end of the world, in time it will become but a distant memory.

Analyze what you can learn from what has happened. If it's job-related, do you need to redo your CV, or get more work experience? Were you paralyzed with nerves? In which case, practice interview techniques. Make sure you are thoroughly prepared for next time, so that you can sell yourself and your skills. Remind yourself that sometimes interviews are just a process a company goes through and the job could be already allocated to an internal candidate.

If a piece of work goes badly wrong and gets a lot of criticism, listen carefully to what has been said. Did you really do your best? Could you have done more? Once the first sting of hurt has passed, you can learn from this feedback. If you genuinely feel out of your depth, perhaps you are not in the right place or position and the work doesn't use your skill sets, in which case you would do better to move on. There is no shame in that — it's an intelligent, considered redirection.

A bad romance is heart-breaking, but do you really want to waste too much time pining for someone who didn't appreciate or value you? You deserve better, keep telling yourself that and <u>move on</u>.

#50 Thank your mother and father

Imagine you wake after 30 minutes sleep to the sound of a screaming baby. The baby is 24 hours old and you do not know what the #?@! you are doing. You consult the manuals, you change nappies, you feed, you burp, to no avail. You repeat the whole process again and again. After three hours screaming the baby falls asleep, and so do you, for 30 short minutes, until the baby reawakens and the whole cycle repeats again, and again! This is parenthood. It's the hardest and the most joyous experience in life, and nothing prepares you for it.

You may not realize what your parents did for you (and them) until you have a child of your own. The clouds will lift, and you will begin to understand them. That is the point when you want to give your mum/dad/carer the biggest hug and say thank you! Sometimes, that moment comes too late. So, say it now.

Thank you

I would like to thank my children, Hattie and George, my husband Vaughan, and Renata who witnessed it all. Jane Eastoe helped considerably with the text and Katrina Fray did much of the early research work. All errors are mine.

Bella Cockrell and Michelle Mac pulled the project together. And Laura Quick put her wonderful illustrations to the words — thank you.

First published in the United Kingdom in 2019 by
Pavilion
43 Great Ormond Street
London, WC1N 3HZ

ISBN 978-1-91162-433-2

A CIP catalogue record for this book is available from the British Library.

10 9 8 7 6 5 4 3 2 1

Reproduction by Rival Colour Limited, UK
Printed and bound by 1010 Printing International Ltd, China

www.pavilionbooks.com

Prevent Breast Cancer Ltd.
Registered Charity No: 1109839
Registered in England No: 4831397

prevent breast cancer